Albertina Georgette Joe

BIOGRAPHY
of
SISTER ALBERTINA GEORGETTE JOE

and Memoirs of Cole Bay Village

Agnes Aventurin

XULON PRESS

Xulon Press
555 Winderley Pl, Suite 225
Maitland, FL 32751
407.339.4217
www.xulonpress.com

© 2022 by Agnes Aventurin

Edited by Xulon Press

All rights reserved solely by the author. The author guarantees all contents are original and do not infringe upon the legal rights of any other person or work. No part of this book may be reproduced in any form without the permission of the author.

Due to the changing nature of the Internet, if there are any web addresses, links, or URLs included in this manuscript, these may have been altered and may no longer be accessible. The views and opinions shared in this book belong solely to the author and do not necessarily reflect those of the publisher. The publisher therefore disclaims responsibility for the views or opinions expressed within the work.

Unless otherwise indicated, Scripture quotations taken from the King James Version (KJV) – *public domain*. (also GW) Scripture quotations taken from the Gods Word Translation copyright ©1995 by Baker Publishing Group. Scripture quotations taken from the Holy Bible, New International Version (NIV). Copyright © 1973, 1978, 1984, 2011 by Biblica, Inc.™. Used by permission. All rights reserved. Scripture quotations taken from the New Revised Standard Version (NRSV). Copyright © 1989 the Division of Christian Education of the National Council of the Churches of Christ in the United States of America.

Paperback ISBN-13: 978-1-66286-884-9
Hard Cover ISBN-13: 978-1-66286-885-6
Ebook ISBN-13: 978-1-66286-886-3

Table of Contents

Chapter 1: Albertina's Story 1
  Miracle child 1
  Family life 3
  Difficult times during World War II 9
  Stone Ovens 9
  Grocery Shops in Cole Bay............................. 12
  James Laveist aka "Uncle Jim" Albertina's
  favorite uncle.. 14
  Albertina's favourite time of the year................ 15
  Appliances used before the Dawn of Electricity in
  Sint Maarten.. 16
  Education... 19
  The arrival of Princess Juliana in 1944 and Sint Maarten's
  first Airport... 22
  Where Albertina got the name "Teacher" 24
  Sewing classes, and a Narrative Behind Albertina's
  teachers 27
  Albertina, and her music class teacher 29
  The Cole Bay Methodist Church 30
  Albertina, Cole Bay Methodist Church school teacher and
  leader of the Young Adventures group 32
  Organist in the Cole Bay Methodist Church............. 34
  Lucille Hazel (Pioneer of the Women's League) 36

The Church and the Church bell were a resource to the
community of Cole Bay and its environment. 41
Responsibilities. 43
Albertina never married 44
Domestic worker. 45
Past times. 46
Horrible Memories 50
Albertina Joe Hospitalised 51
Awarded for working many years for government and
honored in Cole Bay Methodist Church. 52
Albertina Joe's Family Tree: 54

Chapter 2: Some names of Ministers, Local Preachers, church school Teachers, and students during Albertina's tenure 55

Ministers 55
Local preachers 57
Church School Teachers 57
Church School Students 57

Chapter 3: Some History of Methodism in Sint Maarten 59

Cole Bay Methodist Church. (The Bedrock) 59
Louisiana Illidge, "Mother of Methodism," and 11
churches 61
Highlights of Methodism in Cole Bay 62

Chapter 4: Some Historical Information about St. Maarten 65

The Dawn of Electricity in Sint Maarten 67

Chapter 5: Cole Bay, a Close-Knit Population....... 69

Chapter 6: My story about Sis. Albertina Joe a.k.a. "Teacher"...77

Dedication

For my precious loving mom Clementina Aventurin Powell, my dear sister Elvia and my beloved son, Juancho who has and will always live in our hearts, and to my Primary School teacher, Mr. Camille Baly AKA "Meneer Baly" who encouraged me to write.

Acknowledgment

This small publication would not have been possible without the assistance of Albertina Joe, Neville Lake, Godwin James, Mona Joe, Elcita Atkins, and Felicia James who shared their memories with me.

The staff at the Museum St. Maarten made it possible for me to broaden my research, while Carlos Patrick, former head of the Land registry office in Backstreet Philipsburg, helped me with maps.

Thanks to my sisters, Elmora Aventurin Pantophlet, and my brother-in-law, Antonio Pantophlet, Mary Renfurm, and Elvia Aventurin, (deceased) for encouraging me to do this biography with a little background history of Cole Bay: and to my sister-in-law, Victoria Borg O'Flaherty, for her ideas to make this an interesting book.

To my daughter Zenobia Cannegieter, and granddaughters Nicole and Zénia Cannegieter, for their patience while I worked on completing this book.

Preface

As a child growing up in Cole Bay on the island of St. Maarten, I knew many people who contributed to this community and have since left us. Their legacy lives on, but their knowledge has been buried in the sand in Cay Bay cemetery: such people includes Teclo Pedro Bell, Mildred Richardson, Sylvio Lammar (a.k.a Phelps), Leopold Bell and his wife (former school bus driver, and businessman), Osborn Kruythoff (self-appointed traffic policeman), Hubert Peters, also known as Papa (blacksmith), the Maccows (owner of a grocery store and bakery), our local midwives Elfreida Peters aka Miss Flee, wife of the late Deputy Milton Peters, and Clementina Salomon: The grandmother of Ann Meyers, Elwaldo Richardson (agriculture and concrete block maker), and my dearly beloved mother, Clementina Powell-Aventurin (a domestic aid and entrepreneur), and many others.

Nothing much has been documented about the old traditions of the Cole Bay Methodist Church, or the life of these persons in Cole Bay. We tend to read and learn about people who came to us from abroad, but the stories of our Cole Bay people were never told. Albertina Joe is one of the last remaining stalwarts of that generation and is still with us in the Cole Bay Methodist Church. Her story can shed some light on how the Church has been a source of inspiration in our community. She has left an everlasting impression on me since childhood. When I listen to her, I remember a sentence in the book *Disciple: Becoming Disciples through Bible Study* by Richard Byrd Wilke and Julia Kitchens Wilke, which says, **"God uses the simple to show faith and love". (ISBN 13: 978-0-687-78349-6 Study Manual, copyright 1993 by Abingdon Press)**

The idea of writing this biography came about some years ago, when a pastor of our Congregation, celebrated her birthday and the members had a big performance for her at church. The pastor had only been with us for five months, and the members were honouring her with flowers and rendered items. This was a very good idea; it made her feel loved and welcomed, but the members forgot a stalwart of the church who has toiled unendingly in this community. She, too, celebrated her birthday on that same day, but no provision was made for her, not even a song to honour her. I realised that when persons are no longer active in the public eye, they and their contributions are quickly forgotten. I would like our young people to know this lovely lady as an enterprising, committed, and ambitious person who loved children and lived her life all for the Glory of God.

Chapter 1

Albertina's Story

Albertina Joe was born on the island of Curaçao in the St. Elisabeth Hospital on February 22nd, 1932. She was the daughter of the late Ernest and Leonora Joe of St. Maarten and sister of the late Eulalie Joe, who lived in the United States for forty years.

Miracle child
Leonora Joe was very ill during her pregnancy and the doctors at the St. Rose Hospital in Sint Maarten, which was then situated in Philipsburg, Backstreet, could not take care of her, so they sent her to Curacao.

In those days, there wasn't any airport, so people travelled by boat for approximately five days from St. Maarten to Curaçao. According to Carlos Patrick, Kennedy Thompson, and Edwin Philips, a.k.a. Nokky, the boats that traversed back and forth between St. Maarten, Curaçao, Bonaire, Saba, and St. Eustatius were the *Kralendijk*, *Ruth*, *Godfield*, *Cerena* and the *Willemstad*.

The plan was that as soon as Leonora Joe, a.k.a. Miss Lilly, was ready to deliver her baby in Curaçao, the doctors would take the child by caesarean section, for there was a chance that the birth could endanger her life. After the infant was born, she, too, became very ill. They were both far from home, and despite all types of treatments, the doctors found that they were not having the results they wanted. In the end, they gave up on the baby and told Leonora that there was nothing more they could do for her child; they fully expected that she was going to die. By then, the frail Albertina was eleven months old and, on hearing the medical prognosis, her mother decided to bring her child back to St. Maarten so that her father would at least see her while she was still alive.

When I interviewed Albertina, she was an energetic and witty seventy five year old woman. It is no wonder that her family called her a miracle child; a name she gladly embraced, as she was fully aware of the obstacles her fragile life slowly overcame in infancy. "I'm a miracle child. God wanted me here for a reason and that reason is for Him. He said, 'I want you to do some work for me while here on earth, so I won't take you now. I need you for a while to do something for Me, and this is why I am trying. I want to be faithful until the end of my days, I really want to be. I am just like Ruth from the Bible; I am faithful to God," Albertina explained.

Albertina and mother

Family life

Albertina's parents raised animals for a living. They kept sheep, goats, pigs, and chickens, which they sold to butchers locally and to those who came from neighbouring islands, especially St. Barths. (These people were known as the Cha Chas, and they were descendants of French settlers on that island: (the only group in the Caribbean to have maintained the old French language, traditions, and ethnicity). The family also planted fruits and vegetables on their property, which made it possible for Albertina's parents to purchase shoes, clothes, and whatever else the family might have needed. Shoes were prized possessions and had to be cared for and made to last because they were expensive. "I had a shoe for school and one for church. When we were children, we would go barefooted to the well to fetch water for the animals to drink and or play in the yard," recalled Albertina.

Sources said that in those days, there were not many stores in Philipsburg, or then called Great Bay. Families often relied on parcels of goods, or clothes from relatives who had left the island and were living abroad. The main store owners in Great Bay were Mr. Melford Hazel's, Mrs. Cyrus Wathey, who sold clothing, shoes, and other stationary supplies; and Mrs. Rita Nadal, who had one of the biggest stores on the Front Street. This store was situated on the site now occupied by the Sea View Hotel, but in that store, you could purchase a variety of other supplies.

Albertina and her sister learned from an early age to help around the farm. "I was a shepherdess," Albertina laughingly claimed, and then went on to talk about the places where she took the animals to graze. Every morning before she went to school, she took the sheep anywhere they could feed: these places included Tom Ben's place and the Eli Fleming Grass piece.

Tom Ben's Estate was overgrown with shrubs, fruit trees, cacti, suckers, wild vines, Yellowdad, Coralita, and Manchineel trees. There was one ruined, old house built from wood and standing on a brick foundation. The vegetation on the property was thick like a forest, to where one could barely see the house from the street. It was fenced with huge slave walls and barbed wire fence on the top of the walls. Although the entrance of the property was closed off with a big wooden gate from trespassers, people still found ways of entering. They climbed the slave walls and even broke down the barbed wire, so that they could tie their animals there or pick fruits from the trees. When evening came, many persons, especially children, were afraid to pass by the area because of the darkness. One could hardly see their hands in front of them when passing by the estate at night. Cole Bay did not have any electricity when Albertina was growing up, so they used lamps and lanterns until the village got electricity in the late 1960s.

People claimed that the Tom Ben's property was haunted. At times, when passing by on the street, one could hear sounds coming from the windows or doors that were unhooked. That sound was the wind playing with the loosened windows, of course. Presently, there are several buildings on that property and is occupied by the Tackling families.

Many Years ago, a lady went missing and persons whom she was in contact with, remembered where they last saw her. She was on her way home, but never got there. The people from the community got together and started a search for days but did not find her. The search was called off. A few days later, a passer-by thought he heard someone calling from the Tom Ben's property, so everyone got together and began the search again. They found the lady between cacti and suckers untouched. She looked cared for and said cats were bringing her milk to drink when asked how she looked so good.

Eli Fleming grass piece was on the opposite side of Tom Ben's estate and was also fenced in with big slave walls. The property was overtaken by tall grass that, at times, gave passers-by who got too close some serious cuts. This pasture began from the Union Road back to the pond, which is now partially converted into homes and commercial establishments. In the early days, before the area was built up, the grass pieces were occupied by sheep and goats, but mainly cows. According to Mr. Carlos Patrick, the Carty family were the real owners of that property,

The pond is now called The Simpson bay lagoon. Small boats and Yachts occupy the Simpson bay Lagoon. Big Yachts that sails from abroad traverses back and forth in the Lagoon from the open sea through a Drawbridge that joins the villages of Cole Bay and Simpson Bay. This bridge is now called the John Sainsborough Lejuez Bridge. In Albertina's youthful days in order for Cole Bay people and Simpson Bay people to travel back and forth to the inlands they had a small bridge so they could cross the pond and sea. That bridge can still be seen at the back of Atrium Hotel.

Before Eulalie Joe, Albertina's sister, migrated to the United States, she was the one that took the animals to the well in the Well Road to drink water and then took them home; but Albertina never took them so far. When Albertina returned home from School, She relocated the animals which was tied. At about half past five in the afternoon, she would go for the sheep and penned them in their yard on the family property. She then went to the well to fetch water for the animals; which was situated on the opposite side of the road, not far from their home on the Union Road. At times when she was taking the animals home from where they were tied up on Tom Ben's property, her uncle Jim allowed her to give the animals water to drink from his cistern. She said, with a smile on her face," I was Uncle Jim's favourite, and he spoiled me". The Well, close to Albertina's childhood home, was demolished years ago, but one of the three Wells on Well Road is still standing, disappointingly the trough and copper pots are no longer there.

Remains of the Well near the Cole Bay Lagoon
(photo taken by Mr. Franklin Peters)

Copper pot

People took water from any of the wells to wash their clothes, clean their homes or for their animals to drink. There were troughs next to these wells or copper pots, so people could draw water from the wells and fill the troughs with water for the cows to drink. They tied a long rope to a bucket to dip the water from the well. Nowadays, people use a pump, or insert the hose from the water truck, into the well to draw water from them.

Several houses had cisterns, which were built either close to their homes or under the porch to catch rainwater, while others used big oil drums to hold water in for drinking or cooking. Gutters were placed around the edge of the roofs and a spout then directed into the drums or directly into the cistern to retrieve the rainwater. People used this water for drinking, cooking, cleaning, washing, etc. But when the island of St. Maarten was faced with drought, they would resort to Well water to clean their homes and wash the Laundry with. They saved their cistern water for drinking and cooking. Albertina's parents did not own a cistern, so they used to have drums around their home to catch rainwater as many others did. During drought, her family went to "Uncle Jim's" home and fetched buckets of water that they would use to cook and drink. Albertina found Well water to be heavy, as it comes from a spring in the earth and, when used for washing, it would not lather well.

Difficult times during World War II

Albertina said that during the war, life in St. Maarten became more difficult. There was food rationing and the government gave tickets to each family according to the number of persons who were living in a home. These tickets enabled the family to purchase a certain quantity of imported goods, such as flour, butter, cooking oil, and rice, among other things. The reason for doing this is that during the Second World War, battleships were traversing back and forth at sea, thus making it dangerous for the regular ships to deliver goods regularly to the islands. People risked their lives out at sea. During that time a ship was torpedoed causing it to sink, and some people drowned while others swam ashore. Some of the survivors came up right on the Cape Bay shores, while others swam to Philipsburg and some into the shores of Marigot.

Stone Ovens

Miss Lilly and her husband were the only couple that owned a Stone Oven in Cole Bay during Albertina's childhood days, and various people from that community gathered on Saturdays or during Christmas and Easter holidays in her parents' yard to bake bread or pastries. Albertina explained that a Stone Oven is an outdoor oven build from bricks and white stones that were collected from the seaside. When people gathered the stones, they would burn them, then pound them until they became a fine powder, mixing the powder with water until it became like lime or mud. They would lay the bricks with this mud. In her younger days, they used this mixture instead of cement to hold the bricks together. Albertina reminisced on this; "One can imagine how much Timber they gathered from the woods, to keep the Stone Oven hot, so the bread or pastries could have baked properly." She mentioned that neighbours who did not own an oven would ask her mother to bake their cakes and tarts in her stone oven, because they used only cold pots and later on kerosine stoves in those days.

According to Mr. Edwin James, he is of the opinion that Ms. Albertina Joe's family was one of the well-to-do families in Cole Bay. They were businesspeople and catered to many needs. He can remember an incident happened during the time of World War II when a man murdered someone and was locked up in the French prison. He managed to escape and went hiding in the hills. Apparently, the man could see the police and Gendarmes, when they were seeking him, from where he was hiding, but they could not see him. This man remained in the hills for many days. One afternoon, while the Cole Bay people were in the yard waiting for their bread to bake in Miss Lilly's Oven, a heavy shower of rain came down. All gathered, hurried into their home for shelter. When the rain stopped, they went to gather their breads from the oven, but there was hardly any bread in it. Apparently, the fugitive took them out and went back to the hills; however, he was captured very soon after.

Remains of a stone oven taken in the back of Molly Maccow's home on Union Road Cole Bay. (Photos taken by Mrs. Elcitat Reed-Atkins)

Another story about Miss Lilly and her stone oven: One Evening she left a sweet potato pudding in her Stone Oven to finish baking while she went to choir practice at Church, and there was no pudding in the Oven when she returned home. Seemingly, some young boys took it out of the Oven, consumed it and placed the pan with water back into the Oven. Sources say she was fuming mad.

Grocery Shops in Cole Bay

Albertina remembered purchasing groceries from Mr. van Buren James' parent's grocery shop. This shop was located on Union Road, opposite where their family grocery shop is currently. The Shop was managed from one of the rooms in a part of their family home and was controlled from through a window. People purchased goods from through a window while standing outside of the building. Items such as butter, lard, cheese, sausage, rice, or flour were purchased by ounce (onz), pound (lb.) or kilo.

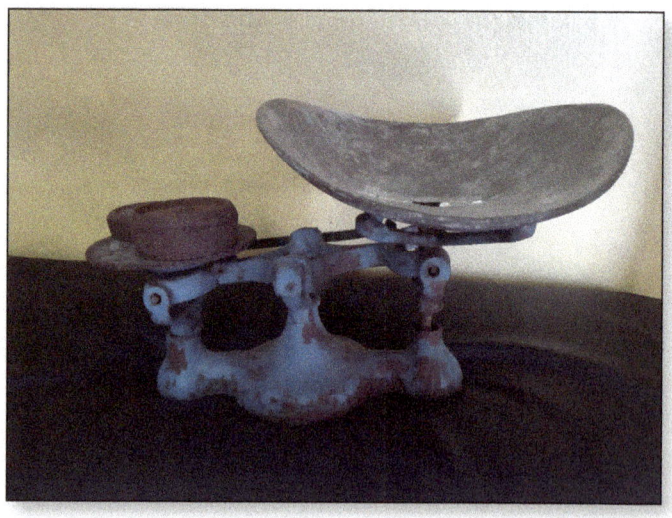

Scales and weights

Albertina Joe clearly remembered another small shop further down the street around where Kentucky presently is located on the Well-fair Road. but, could not remember who owned it. (I later found out that the Shop belonged to Businessman Mr. Leopold Bell and His wife before they relocated on Union Road, Cole Bay.) She said "after window shopping was through, it was over-the-counter shopping. Persons requested what they needed from over the counter until modern time; now one can go and pick up whatever they need from the shelves and advance to the cashiers to pay for their items". In Albertina's days, the money used amongst other currencies was mainly Dutch Antillean guilders and the shop owners also accepted any currency from the suppliers who did business with them. Be it Spanish, English, French they accepted the money. Now St. Maarten uses guilders, Euros, or US dollars. In the past, people called Twenty five Antillean cents 0'10 cents, and a Ten cent was 0,04 cents. Five cents, was 0,02 cents and two and a half cents was 0,01 cent. The shop keepers threw the 0,01 cents away or never accepted them. Albertina said, "I never understood why it was done that way".

According to sources back in the 1800's and the early 1950's business people such as store owners and farmers kept their money stored in brown paper bag or a cloth bag sewn by they themselves and hid their money either in their Mattress of their beds, in a safe place be it in their homes or buried them in their yard. They did this because, there were no Banks on the island of St. Maarten for persons to deposit their money like these modern times. Before the bank existed shop keepers/ suppliers divided the Antillean guilders by 2.5.

The Windward Island Bank a branch of Maduro & Curiel Bank in Curacao was the first Bank on the island of St. Maarten. This Bank opened its doors to the public on December 01st. 1960. Cited https://www.wib-bank.net History – WIB St. Maarten

James Laveist aka "Uncle Jim"
Albertina's favorite uncle

Albertina and her sister had several uncles and aunts, but James Laveist, better known as Uncle Jim, was her favourite; he was her mother's brother. Uncle Jim lived abroad for a while and He always looked out for them even though he was living and working in Aruba, he never forgot them. He always sent whatever he could put together for her and her sister when he was sending a package to her parents. She said he was a God-fearing man and always gave them good advice. At times, she did not adhere to his warnings, but would quickly find out how right he was. She also said he was honest, showed no partialities, and was always willing to help people. She remembered that while he lived in Aruba, when he wrote to her parents, he always started his letters by quoting a scripture from the Bible. When uncle Jim returned to St. Maarten, he attended Church regularly. He praised

God Almighty in everything that he did until he passed on, Uncle Jim never missed church unless he was very ill. He always sat on the last pew at the back of the Methodist church, with his black hat placed on the floor under the pew while Sunday, Morning Worship was taking place.

Albertina's favourite time of the year

Christmas was Albertina's favourite time of the year when she was a little girl. She used to go with her sister and parents, along with other folks from Cole Bay, through the village all the way to Simpson Bay, carolling from door to door. During this season, people would give them goodies to eat or a glass of homemade drink (drinks such as guava berry, lime punch, or lemonade when they were serenading. These drinks are made from our own local fruits). It was normal for people to go around serenading during the Christmas season and after the serenades finished, the homeowner will share their Christmas treats with them. Most homes who could afford it would always have various punches such as guava berry, lime punch, sorrel, and pomserette punch, which they prepared personally. So was the coconut, guava, guava berry tarts, and pound cake or fruit cakes. She said that her mother used to bake lots of pies, cakes, bread, and tarts in their stone oven for their personal use, as well as to sell during Christmas and Easter time. (Guava Berry is St. Maarten Local drink known worldwide).

Guava Berry drink

Appliances used before the Dawn of Electricity in Sint Maarten

Albertina remembered that as a little child, Kerosine oil was used for lighting Coals for cooking, baking, ironing and also for lighting Lamps and Lanterns at night. There wasn't any fridge to preserve meat, fish, and poultry from spoiling, so they corned most of their fish, beef, and pork meat with cooking Salt and hung them outside to dry until they were ready to be cooked. Chickens were never corned so people kept poultry farms in their back yards. Some of the chickens were kept for laying eggs and the others were slaughtered to eat. There was a different process to prepare fresh Chicken and Fresh meat before it was cooked. Kerosine Refrigerators and Stoves came long after, and only people who could afford them owned one. Kerosine refrigerators were very dangerous in homes because the Wick was left burning all day and night to keep it running and to preserve perishable foods from spoiling. Sources said that many times when they awoke in the morning, the ceilings in their home were under black Soot from the fridge, and it was a job to get it clean, because the wick needed trimming. Very often, persons had to clean the ceiling of their homes and sides of the walls because of the Soot. People cooked on coal pots or outdoor on stones, until hardware stores began selling indoor kerosine appliances here on the island. In earlier days, kerosine stoves and Refrigerators were considered luxury appliances. In order to see at night, persons used kerosine lamps, lanterns, or candles in their homes. Kerosine lamps were also used in church during evening worship, before electricity was introduced. Albertina said that Kerosine Lanterns were hung on the walls of the church and Lamps were used on different tables so people could see during the evening Worship. They also used iron heaters with coal to iron their clothes and, afterward, improved to kerosine or gas heaters to do their ironing.

Flat Iron that held coals on the inside

Flat Iron that was placed on coals to get it heated

Later on gas was an extra benefit to families, people hardly used the kerosine. What we now call an electric heater or iron was once called a 'goose'. Now electricity powers everything, Albertina also mentioned that "electricity has its good and bad qualities: because when she was a young girl, once there was an organist at church there was always music to accompany the congregation while singing, but now a days, once the electricity is off, there is no music unless there is a generator on standby".

Kerosine Lamp

Education

Young Albertina Joe attended the public school in Cole Bay, later named Leonard Conner School, and presently the Charles Leopold Bell School. In those days, there were no kindergarten schools, much less day-cares. She first went to school at the age of six. Her teacher for the first three years was Miss Gertrude Houtman, who taught grades one to three. Her father, Mr. Houtman, taught the other grades. Albertina stopped attending school when she was fourteen years old, but her favourite subject was reading, especially poetry. One of her favourite poems is titled *A Psalm of life* by Henry Wadsworth Longfellow, which suggests that life should be lived as a process of continuous development. At the age of seventy-five, Albertina can still recite it in its entirety.

Her reading grades were always good, and today she proudly remembers that she was one of the best, behaved children in her class. She always got an eight for her behaviour on her report card. "You can bet your last dollar when I took home my report card, it always had Gedrag 8," she said. ("Gedrag" translated into English means behaviour.)

Picture of Leonard Conner school in the past from the Protected Historical sites and buildings on St. Maarten produced by Vromi

Present Leonard Connor School building taken by Sis. Elcita Atkins

Albertina Joe said; The Leonard Connor school in Cole Bay was shut down for a period by the government in Holland, as it was felt that the students were not sufficiently educated in the Dutch language. Therefore, Children walked through short cuts over the hills to get to the public school in Philipsburg. Later on, the government arranged for a school bus to transport the young people to the Oranje School in Philipsburg and back home every day. Albertina said, she could have gone on to seventh grade, but she didn't. She said, "Most of my classmates dropped out of school after we completed the sixth grade and went on to Curacao and Aruba. Some of them went with their parents, and continued their education there. Albertina said she had no notion as to why they travelled abroad.

Sources says that St. Maarten thrived on Sugar, Salt, and the Cotton Industry, and in the early 1900 with the closing down of the Plantations and the slowing down of the salt production, along with the two world wars many unemployed (mostly Fathers) traveled abroad with the hope of a better living for their families. They traveled mainly to the island of Curacao, and Aruba to seek work in the Oil refineries, to the Dominican Republic and Cuba to pursue work in Cane fields and Rice plantations. Apparently, life was rough here on St. Maarten. There were hardly any work, so the fathers of these families travelled abroad to seek work, and when he settled down, the rest of his family joined him. This transition caused St. Maarten to have a decline in a considerable amount of its inhabitants. Statistics shows that from the 4000 inhabitants on the island of St. Maarten approximately 2000 remained during that period. In 1965 the duty-free status, and the many unspoiled white sandy beaches made St. Maarten a popular travel destination. Tourism Industry began to rise, and Families returned to their home in St. Maarten, The population grew rapidly to over 4000 inhabitants in comparison to the 2000 inhabitants that was left in St. Maarten in the 1940's. Albertina and her family were one of those families who never traveled abroad like other families, and stayed in St. Maarten.

Albertina clarified, "These people travelled along with their parents from in the earlies, but I choose to stay in St. Maarten because I wanted to be with Mommy. Now, mommy gone leave me, but I am still around, and I praise God for that." Albertina was thirteen years younger than her sister, so her playmates were Suzanne Reed, her next-door neighbor, and other neighbours. The school did not offer any activities, such as gymnasium or outdoor physical exercise, so they skipped rope, played hide-and-seek and Ring-Around-The-Roses during recess.

The arrival of Princess Juliana in 1944 and Sint Maarten's first Airport

There were no school outings either, however, Albertina and her schoolmates had a field trip for the 1st, time when Princess Juliana made her first visit to St. Maarten in 1944;

she was not yet crowned queen of the Dutch Kingdom. This memorable event took place when Albertina was twelve years old.

She said, "When Princess Juliana visited the island, we dressed up beautifully and traveled to the Airport to welcome the princess and sang. We were adorned with rosettes of red, white and blue, and an orange ribbon from our right shoulder tied by our hips. When the royal plane landed, we began to wave and when the princess exited the plane on her way to the Airport terminal, we sang 'The Dutch Anthem' and other songs while waving our flags. After this event, we returned to school".

She also said, "That was a great experience for me as a child—going to sing for the royal princess."

Research shows that Princes Juliana passed through St. Maarten on her way back to the Netherlands on March 4, 1944. She and her husband, along with their children, traveled from Canada where they lived for a while during the Second World War. The Princess Juliana Airport officially opened on December 3, 1943. KLM Royal Dutch Airlines began weekly flights from Curacao to St. Maarten and back; it heralded the end of the isolation of St. Maarten and the beginning of a new era.

Picture of the 1ˢᵗ Princess Juliana Airport

Where Albertina got the name "Teacher"

The majority of us thought Albertina Joe got the nickname "Teacher" because of the church school. However, it turns out she earned it much earlier. She explained that when she was in the third grade, the class read a book called, *The Improved Reader*, which contained a number of different stories. One of the stories that she loved and inspired her was the one called, "Little Goody Two Shoes". The story is told of a little girl who lived in a faraway land where there were no schools and the population were very poor; however, this little girl's family were a little better off than them, and She could have read and write. One day she mentioned to her parents that she wanted to help children learn to read and write. She then asked her father to encourage parents in the community to send their children to certain locations for her to teach them to read and write. This her father did, and she would go to various areas and teach her students under a tree.

Albertina said, this little girl had one pair of shoes to wear and instead of wearing them on her feet, she held them in her hand while she travelled to different areas to teach the children. This went on for years, until the government constructed a school where she could teach the children. Albertina said this story had a great impact on her life; she asked her parents if they could ask parents in the village of Cole Bay if they would send their four- and five-year-old children to her in the afternoon so she could teach them to read and write. The people were receptive to this, as there was no day-care or kindergarten in those days. People had to work, while their children stayed home alone or with other family members after school until they returned from work.

Albertina said after people began sending their children, she had her father build two long benches for her little students to sit on under the manchineel tree in her parents' yard. If it rained, they would all relocate into the house. As years went by a few grown men and women, who could not read and write also took classes from Albertina. She got her teaching material from the school. She explained, "The school teacher gave me the old small slates they were not using any longer and the little pieces of chalk that was left over in the class to use and my parents bought me a few books from the books store in Philipsburg." Albertina also said, "Once the children started coming, the first thing I told them was 'You all have to call me Teacher from today on'. You hear 'Teacher!"

When her students arrived, they would say "Good afternoon, Teacher" and they addressed her as such throughout the class until they left. After that, they would call her Teacher when passing her on the streets; this name stuck with her until today. "I taught them their ABCs, how to count, identifying the letters of the alphabet and the numbers, nursery rhymes, songs from the Sunday School hymnal, and scripture verses from the Holy Bible. I also taught them words from books that my parents bought me from a bookstore in Philipsburg," Albertina recalls. Her fee for teaching these toddlers was Naf. 0,10 cts. weekly per child, and the parents gladly paid it. Some of her first students were Elaine Richardson, deceased, Everette Richardson, Antonio Samuel, Irwin Richardson (a.k.a Baco, now deceased), Edith Lake, and others. She said as the first set of children got old enough to leave, new ones came, and this went on for years.

A manchineel is a very poisonous tree, which people had planted all over their properties here in St. Maarten. It has been said that the Caribs used the liquid from the trees on the point of their spares to poison their opponents. The tree can reach up to fifteen meters in height and has a greyish bark, shiny green leaves and spikes of small greenish flowers. Its fruit, which is similar in appearance to an apple, are green or greenish-yellow when ripe. The manchineel tree can be found near to and around beaches. It is a good windbreaker and its roots stabilize the sand, preventing beach erosion. They were also used a boundaries to separate properties here on St. Maarten.

Machineel fruits. Resembles small green Apples. They are poisonous.

Sewing classes, and a Narrative Behind Albertina's teachers

Miss Eudene Sharp taught Albertina how to sew. According to Mr. Carlos Patrick, Miss Eudene Sharp was a petite black woman who lived in the Widow's lot in Philipsburg. That's an alley between Front Street and Back Street in the Down Street area, called "Weduwen Straat". It is said that this lot was owned by a wealthy man who left it for widows and single women to occupy. No male was permitted to live on that property with any of those women. There were many fruit trees on this property. On public holidays, especially on Queen's Birthday (April 30th)[1] and St. Maarten's Day (November 11th), Albertina, her mother and her niece (Mona Joe) would travel to Philipsburg (Great Bay) to spend the day by Miss Sharp. They brought along their food baskets so they all could eat and share what they had. According to sources, there were two other single ladies who occupied the lot; one being Miss Treling. According to Mr. Neville Lake, Miss Eudene Sharp was qualified as a woman in high standing. Although highly educated and being a great seamstress, she suffered discrimination and was never accorded the recognition she deserved for her skills because she was a dark brown-skinned female.

Albertina also had some sewing lessons from Mrs. Leontine Maccow (deceased) in Cole Bay, who was the wife of Mr. Assie Emanuel Maccow (deceased) and the mother of eleven children. The family's property is on Union Road, past the corner towards the left of the basketball Court and the Leonard Conner School, on the way to Marigot, French St. Martin. Their garden was always well-kept, with a very large, flamboyant tree in the centre of the garden. (The flamboyant tree is one of the national flowers of St. Maarten and many people have one planted in their yards.)

---

[1] Queen Juliana's birthday was celebrated yearly on April 30th.

The Flamboyant Tree. The national tree of Sint Maarten.

Sewing was one of Albertina's other hobbies, as she sewed and took pleasure in making clothes for her family and friends, but she never made a career of it.

Albertina, and her music class teacher

Miss Agatha Wathey, who lived on Front Street, on the left property of the Philipsburg Methodist Church, was young Albertina's piano teacher. Albertina practised piano for quite some years and learned enough to enable her to play and lead the choir in the Cole Bay Methodist Church. Ms. Agatha Wathey was the organist and choir conductor in the Philipsburg Methodist Church in the early thirties and forties. Later Albertina, herself, was to teach young people to play the piano at her home in Cole Bay.

The Cole Bay Methodist Church

Albertina's involvement in the Cole Bay Methodist Church started early. She accepted the Lord at the age of fourteen, but said, "I already knew I loved the Lord before I got confirmed and became a member of the Cole Bay Methodist Church". She took on numerous tasks and devoted her time to the church. She was the organist, a Sunday school teacher, choir conductor, leader of the Young Adventures, and the domestic worker of the church. Teacher also visited the sick at their homes and assisted the pastor with administering the sacrament to the shut-in members of the Cole Bay Methodist Church. She commented, while smiling, "I was very faithful and dependable. The church could count on me. Once I gave you my word, you could believe it was done".

The Cole Bay Methodist Church was the first Methodist Church founded on the island of St. Maarten. The two-story wooden structure was erected in 1925. Consequently, Members from Simpson Bay, and other members from both Dutch and French sides of the island worshipped in the Cole Bay Methodist Church. Sis. Louise Halley said that her God mother Miss Rose Peterson (deceased) told her that Simpson Bay and Cole Bay Village were separated by the Sea and Pond water when they were children. So, the members from Simpson Bay travelled via a Rowboat to Worship on Sundays with the members of Cole Bay Methodist Church. The boat docked where the Tropicana Casino is at present.

The present Cole Bay Methodist Church.
Photo taken by Zénia Cannegieter

Albertina cleaned the church every Saturday and placed a fresh bouquet of flowers from her parent's garden on the communion table, every Sunday morning. She rendered all these services without charging a penny. As a little girl growing up, Albertina's Church School teacher was her godmother, Sister Alice David. When Albertina became a Church School teacher, she taught the Sunday school children Bible verses, songs and Bible stories, Bible quizzes, and when they returned the following Sunday, they had to repeat what they learned the week before so she could go on to another lesson.

She also taught the children poems and skits for Christmas, Mother's Day, Father's Day, Easter, and Harvest. She prepared the young people for quiz competitions between the other Methodist Congregations and with a big smile on her face expressed herself proudly: "and you better believe it, Cole Bay Methodist Scholars always won first prize." Sometimes Albertina also took part in Bible plays, such as the stories of Ruth and Esther. Her first Sunday School students were Mona Joe, Linda Piper-Peters (a.k.a Tatty), Cynthie Richardson, Doris Payne, Ruth Nisbeth, Cynthia Nisbeth, Diane Bell, and others. Erma and her sister Monica Richardson and Vernice David smilingly admitted that Albertina taught her scholars so well that when there were competitions in the circuit, you could believe Cole Bay Methodist Church School scholars always won first prize.

Albertina, Cole Bay Methodist Church school teacher and leader of the Young Adventures group

Although Albertina had no children of her own, she always loved children. This was displayed from an early age when she would teach toddlers under a tree in her parents' yard. Albertina almost quit teaching at the Church School because she was the only teacher despite the increasing number of students. The pastor had repeatedly asked for volunteers, but no one was willing to assist. Every time she threatened to leave, her mother and others would encourage her to continue. Albertina said; "my mother always prayed to God to strengthen me and to give me the will to carry on, and an old lady from another denomination also prayed relentlessly for me. Especially when my mom was getting down in age."

This went on until Sisters' Adina Bell and Mildred Rochester started giving their time to the Church School. Albertina was the Godmother of several children just to mention a few; Annie and Chlorisia Gumbs, Louis Laveist, George and Ingrid Reed, Angelica Richardson, Serge Gumbs, Wilfred Richardson, and Donald Mathew.

Albertina explained that the Young Adventures were a group of young ladies between the ages of eight and fourteen, who met once weekly at the church to do Bible study, learn hymns, do Bible quizzes, do drills and take part in outdoor activities. When the Church members decided to build a Recreation Hall at the back of the Church building, she had the Young Adventures gather stones and gravel as their contribution towards constructing the building. For years, the hall was used as a public kindergarten school, a Methodist School, Sunday School and recreational events until it was destroyed by fire. A new hall was constructed in 2006. It's a 2-story building and it is used for Social events, for Concerts, inhouse meetings and Public meetings as well, Church School, Soup Kitchen program, Feeding less-fortunate persons in our community and its environment through a Pantry. This procedure is still happening today. At times Classes from the regular Schools are still held there.

*Teacher at the ground-breaking of the new church Hall.
Foto by Berthille Chittick.*

Sisters Erma and Monica Richardson were two of the members of the Young Adventures amongst other young people. Sister Monica said we had to be ready for every time teacher Albertina was on her way going to teach Sunday School, or to the Young Adventure meetings. Our mother always looked out for when she was nearing our home on her way to the Church and would tell us, "Teacher is coming, go and join her."

Organist in the Cole Bay Methodist Church

Albertina Joe started playing the organ in the church at the age of twenty, after her sister migrated to the United States. She explained, "After my sister migrated to the United States, everyone expected me to take over where she had left off." At first, I felt incapable taking on such a responsibility, but after lots of persuasion from others, I mastered the courage to try it." She said; in those days, the church did not have an electronic organ. This meant I had to peddle the organ with my feet while I was playing, or no sound would come from the instrument. This I did three times on Sundays: during the Morning and Evening Church Services, and during church school at three o'clock in the afternoon. I also played the Organ during the weekly Worship and for Choir practice, or any other occasion, such as funerals or weddings. Evening services took place under the light of lamps and lanterns. This continued until electricity was installed in the church and the organ was changed."

Albertina said sadly; "If I could play the piano by ear, I would still render my services to the church; unfortunately, I can only read notes."

She also mentioned. "On Friday evenings, the Church Choir would practice Introit hymns, Offerty hymns, the Ancient hymns and canticles and other hymns. I was their leader and conductor.

She stated: "The duty of the Church choir is to know the hymns and lead the Congregation in song. Especially songs the congregation is not familiar with. Some of the words in the hymnal would suit the message God's messenger presented. Sometimes the Minister might request the Congregation to sing a hymn that the tune was unknown, to the members. That is where the Choir would chime in. That is one of the choir's purpose".

She said; "The Church Choir is also a ministry; some people can be converted by the words from a song, a prayer, and/or the words from the pastor or local preachers". She also explained *The Magnificat* and other songs came from the Bible, but the persons who put the hymnals together inserted them in the back of the hymnals for us to chant them. The Minister or the local preacher assigned to preach gave me the hymns to be sung during the Sunday morning worship, before service began. And I continued doing this until my sight began failing me".

Lucille Hazel (Pioneer of the Women's League)

Albertina was also a member and the secretary of the Women's League. Sister Lucille Hazel, (deceased) A.K.A "Miss Lou," was the person instrumental in forming the league in Cole Bay Methodist Church. She lived abroad for many years and came back to settle home, (Sint Maarten) bringing new ideas to the Cole Bay Methodist Church; and, before long, all Methodist churches on the island started a Women's League and it still exists today.

Picture of Lucille Hazel photo by Mr. van Buren James

Lucille Hazel James – Pioneer-Women's League on St. Maarten

So then, my dear sisters, stand firm and steadfast, unmovable, always in your work for the Lord, since you know that nothing you do in the Lord's name is ever without value.

Mrs. Lucille Hazel - James started the first women's league group in 1947 at the Cole Bay Methodist Church. She had the foresight to organize the group and the commitments to work within the Church and the wider community.

- She recognized that the society was changing and that the needs of women were also changing.
- She recognized that women's roles were widening, not as just mothers, homemakers but as career women as well.

Therefore it was necessary for women to learn to balance home, family, the workplace and their Faith.

The women who became members of the Women's League exemplified the above in their lives and sought to teach other women by example and by practical activities.

This progressive Methodist Church Organisation, has grown since those early days and can be found in all the Methodist Congregations in both circuits on the island.

- 1947 – Cole Bay Congregation
- 1948 – Bethel Congregation
- 1948 – Philipsburg Congregation (September 19th.)

Documentary on the women's League taken from the Philipsburg Methodist Church office gallery.

Miss Lou Hazel taught Albertina how to take minutes during meetings. Albertina said; "I was always working in the church and at one time, Miss Lou Hazel decided that I needed to get away for a while on a little vacation. So, all the members started raising funds so I could take a vacation." Albertina smilingly said, "I was always busy doing something, never travelled abroad, so this was my first time I went away." Albertina travelled to Curaçao, the island where she was born.

Albertina visited the homes of the shut-in members along with, Reverend Wilby. This took place once monthly in the afternoon. Besides visitation, the pastor administered the Holy Sacrament to the members. She said that Reverend Wilby, was affectionately called "Willerby", and was a very nice pastor who encouraged families with positive advice. Tuesday nights was Evening Worship as well, so after they had finished visiting shut-ins throughout the village and its surroundings, he spent the rest of his afternoon at their home chit chatting and sometimes playing the piano until it was time for him to conduct Tuesday, Evening Worship. He stayed by us because the Manse was situated in Philipsburg on the present Philipsburg Methodist Church Grounds. (The Circuit office, and School administration is presently occupying that space.) "Boy! She said: he could play the piano lovely, and smilingly added, "he played by ear'.

Photo of Rev. Frank Wilby "Willerby" and Mrs. Wilby.

Albertina's favourite hymn from the Methodist hymnal # nr. 538: "*What a friend we have in Jesus.*" Author: Joseph Medlicott Scriven, 1820-86, Page 206. Her favourite scripture in the Bible is Psalm 121: "*I will lift up mine eyes unto the hills, from whence cometh my help.*" (KJV) She loves the story of Ruth; "What I loved about Ruth is her faithfulness to her mother in law Naomi; "Albertina said, When Naomi sent her two daughters in law back to her people, Oprah went, but Ruth refused to leave her mother-in-law's side and through her faithfulness, good came to her. She received many blessings from God". She loves Ruth 1:16-17, which she quoted:

> *Entreat me not to leave thee, or to return from following after thee; for wither thou goest, I will go, and when thou lodges, I will lodge, thy people shall be my people and thy God my God. Where thou diest, will I die, and there will I be buried. The Lord do so to me, and more also, if ought but death past thee and me.* (King James Version)

Albertina said she once took part in the play of Ruth and acted as Ruth. She also likes a book entitled *Basket of Flowers*, written by Christoph Von Schmid, and she believes that every young person should read this book. "It teaches you to live honestly, to be truthful, not to envy anyone, and to trust God, For whatever He has in store for you it will fall right in your lap."

The Church and the Church bell were a resource to the community of Cole Bay and its environment

Albertina was also one of the persons who rang the church bell. She said that when someone from the village died, Brother Gerald Richardson, Sister Adina Bell, or herself went to the church and tolled the bell. This way, the villagers were made aware that someone had passed from this community. Teacher said the community was small and when they heard the bell ring at an unusual time of course, they knew someone had passed. Tolling of the bell for a funeral had a different sound than the usual way the bell rang. Now, during funerals, the bell rang before the coffin (Casket) entered the church. This was a sort of way to let everyone know the dead had arrived and was about to enter the church. When the funeral Service was over, the bell rang once then paused alternately. (Tolling the bell). After a moment of ringing, and after a short wait, the person tolling the bell waited for a minute or two and pulled on the bell again. This process continued until the funeral procession went out of sight.

Cole Bay Methodist Church original Bell.
Photo taken by Zénia Cannegieter

Albertina recalled the process during funerals from the homes to the Chapel, and from the Chapel to the Cemetery when she was a little girl. She said:

"During funeral processions in my childhood days, there were no transportation to take the corpse in the casket to the Chapel nor to the cemetery, and there were no funeral homes either." So, four (4) persons would walk with a chair each; two on the right and two at the left of the casket. When the bearers, carrying the casket to the Cape Bay cemetery on foot, got tired, they would place the coffin on the chairs while they rested. This went on until they reached the cemetery. Wakes were held to keep the family company at night, while the corpse was laid out in their home until it was buried. The relatives, friends, and visitors were served with soda biscuits, tea and/or coffee. Hymns were sung and passages from the Bible were read, while some people played dominoes. When transportation was introduced, Gerald Richardson would toll the bell while the pallbearers were entering and leaving the church, this would go on until the transport turned the corner of Union Road, Cole Bay on the way to the Cay Bay cemetery.

Sister Albertina, Brother Gerald, or Sister Adina tolled the bell around eight every Sunday morning, and around ten o' clock, at least a half hour before Sunday Morning Worship began. In those days, Sunday Morning Worship began at 10.30 a.m. and lasted an hour and a half. At 9 in the morning, The bell reminded the people Morning Worship would commence later and when hearing it for the second time, they knew Service was about to begin within the next half hour. One of them tolled the bell again in the Evening before the seven p.m. Service commenced. The other time the bell would ring was for weddings. Many years ago, the Church remained open all day long. No one went in to vandalize or steal anything. Persons use to enter the Church to kneel and pray. Regrettably, because of increased crime in the area, churches are kept closed when it is not occupied.

Responsibilities

Albertina's father Ernest Joe died when she was sixteen years old. It was a big blow to the family, but the girls and their mother pulled together and survived as best they could. Two years later, her sister Eulalie gave birth to a daughter and named her Mona Joe. Eulalie was sent to the United States of America and left her baby with her mother and sibling. Albertina helped her mother take care of the baby and was the first person to take Mona for an early morning walk. She said the older folks used to say whenever you are taking a baby out for an early morning walk you should head to the East, so she did that every morning once the weather permitted. She would begin her walk from their home on Union Road up to the Tamarind tree, just before the corner in Cole Bay and back. (The tamarind tree is still standing.)

Albertina never married
Marriage was not in the books for Albertina, as she continued to devote herself to her immediate family and church family. Her mother, Miss Lily, was confined to bed for many years and became quite helpless. Fortunately, she was a small lady and Albertina looked after her as best she could. Elcita Reed Atkins, recalls when she was a little girl that she or her sister stayed many times with Miss. Lilly, while Albertina went to work or did her errands. Ms. Suzanne Reed was a childhood friend of Albertina. She also recalled Miss Lilly being very dependent on others that when she was tired of lying on one side, she would ask one of them to turn her the other way. Albertina explained, "My only sister went to live in the U.S.A. When I had things to do or had to go out, I would always look for someone to stay with her until

I returned." Thinking back on that time, she exclaimed, "I feel like I can move mountains," and, quoting from Hymn 390 of the Methodist Hymnal, she continued, "*Give me the faith that can remove, and sink the mountains to a plain; give me the child-like praying love, which longs to build Thy house again.*"

Domestic worker

Albertina was a government employee for over twenty-five years, working for a living at the Leonard Conner School, now named Charles Leopold Bell School. She said, "I used to go out to make my little change. I worked at the school every afternoon, Monday to Friday after school concluded at one o'clock, cleaning toilets, sweeping, mopping floors and cleaning desks in the class rooms. I wasn't ashamed to do that at all." Teacher also got recognition for the work she carried out from her employer on several occasions. Elcita Reed-Atkins, her neighbour said, "Teacher really worked hard to put food on the table and to keep her mother comfortable. Besides all the things she did at the church and her job, she did a lot at home." She also remembers Albertina picking Plums and selling them when they were ripe. Mr. Frank Arnell said when he was a young man, his parents were good customers of Albertina. When Plum season came around, she would save their Bags of Plums for them. After a while, they did not have to order any, for she kept theirs for them as they were good customers. He said she sold the

Plums for Naf. 0,25 cents per bag. Albertina said they had fields of Plum trees on their property."

Past times

Even in her younger days, Albertina loved to read. Mona, her niece, found her to be a good storyteller: she said" when my aunt told a story, if it was a sad one, listeners were bound to feel the sadness and even cry, and if it was one to be happy, they would feel the joy because, she could have drawn anyone into a story. She continued to say, One of my Aunt's favourite story was *"The Basket of Flowers"*. The way she told it, she would have people glued to their seats. "This was one of the stories that would have you crying at one time and then happy the other," Mona recalled.

Albertina also loved gardening. She liked to plant fruit trees, vegetables or Flower trees and enjoyed their produce. She said, "Trees make the place feel breezier". One day she managed to reap a very big pumpkin from her garden.

Albertina posing with one of her many pumpkins she reaped from her vegetable garden.

She explained: "I planted pumpkin seeds and reaped huge pumpkins, but there was this huge one I even took a picture of, but I can't find that one." Although Albertina had problems with her sight, she still planted. She proudly said, "I am the one who planted my nieces' garden with the fruit trees and plants." Albertina still washed and ironed her own clothing, and cooked for herself at times. She said, "Not that I have to do it, you know, sometimes I feel I want too. Albertina said: of all the cakes I know how to make, I love a pineapple up-side-down cake most of all, and my favourite food is locreo."[2] She said "if I don't have locreo on

---

[2] A dish of chicken, vegetables and herbal seasoning added to rice. It is called pelau elsewhere

my birthday, I will never feel it's my birthday". Albertina loved children and every time her birthday came around; she invited mostly children to her home and celebrated it with them. She played music, and they danced, sang, played games, ate, drank, and was merry. Since Albertina's eyesight failed her, she listened to a Radio Station that aired Bible readings, in addition to what she heard during Sunday Morning Worship Services. Her favorite Radio Station was PJD2. "Proclaiming Jesus Deliverance To You." This Radio Station started transmitting on December 23rd 1959 and was formerly situated on the Fort on Divi Little Bay Hill. Sources said that after the Fort was not used for its original purpose, it was used as a section of the government office for some time and, later, as the Signal Master Station. This commercial Radio Station was managed by Brother Bob Mare and occupied from the other side of the building. It broadcasted religious programs such as Hymns, the Word of God, Bible readings, children's programs, and Local and International News. As history shows, it was at that Fort that Dutch Commander Peter Stuyvesant lost his leg in a sea battle with the Spanish in 1644.

He lost his feet by A stray Spanish cannonball.

The signal Master houses where Radio SXM first begun on the Fort. Protected Historical sites and buildings on St. Maarten produced by Vromi

Albertina reminisced how at 6 pm every afternoon, there was an hour of story time program for children on PJD2 Radio Station and all the children assembled close to the radio to listen to children time. The manner the stories were aired for children one would feel they were actually seeing the individual actors performing. She said stories such as *the little red hen, Puff and tooth, The Troll, Sorry is and Sorry does* were told and felt alive to her. She loved the little choruses they aired and was saddened when story time was about to end. You would hear the speaker close off by singing a lullaby and then saying goodnight. She mentioned: "When television arrived on the island, it was aired only for a couple of hours daily and concluded at a certain hour in the evenings. "Many people were happy to have television and started watching it, but I was never interested in it. I continued listening to the radio and continued reading books." Albertina listened every morning to a program called; *Moments with the Master* aired by Vance James Jr. (deceased). PJD2 is now located on Backstreet, owned By businessman Mr. Donald Hughes.

Horrible Memories

Albertina's most horrible memory was during Hurricane Frederick on September 3rd, 1979. She reminisced about hurricane Frederick being powerful, and that the wind gusts kept rocking their small wooden home back and forth and banging on it endlessly, to where she started losing faith because the wind might not cease before it destroyed their home. She kept praying to God for the wind to stop, because the house started cracking and if the wind did continue, the house would have disintegrated. Her mother was not doing well, health wise, at that time and as she moved around, she fell. Then Albertina tripped and fell on her. She said, "Can you imagine how that had been, my mother and I on the floor struggling, trying to get up, while the strong winds and rain were lashing the house and had it swinging from one side to the other, along with us in it? I was never so frightened in my entire life. I thought the wind was never going to end; we prayed relentlessly, but it seemed the heavy wind was never going to stop, but luckily it stopped on time. Girl! we thanked the Lord so much for saving us."

Two Hurricanes hit the island in succession that year: Hurricane David during the night of Wednesday 29th to Thursday 30 of August, then came Frederick a week later on September 3rd, 1979. Both caused enormous damage on St. Maarten. Hurricane Frederick had winds gusting at 70 km, heavy rains, and even some tornados. Fishing boats sank, and seven deaths were reported.

(Cited from Hurricanecentral.freeservers.com)

Albertina Joe Hospitalised

In 1985, Albertina became ill and was admitted to the St. Rose Hospital for two weeks, but when she was not getting any better, she was sent to Curacao for more treatment. She was hospitalised and treated there for another three weeks, and then returned to St. Maarten. However, she still wasn't feeling any better, so her sister came to St. Maarten and took her to the United States of America for further medical treatment. While there, Eulalie Joe also took her to an eye specialist so that he could check her failing eyesight, but he said it was too late for an operation. She stayed in the United States for another six months and then returned home, still not feeling any better. When she returned to St. Maarten, her niece Mona Joe took care of her until she felt better. Albertina said her niece resided then in Middle Region and she did not attend church very often during that period, but during Hurricane Luis, the house in Middle region was damaged badly, So, she, Mona and her children, returned to Cole Bay to live. Albertina recuperated and started back going out to Church. But, did not take on anymore tasks in church after her illness.

Awarded for working many years for government and honored in Cole Bay Methodist Church

Albertina Joe received gifts and awards on two occasions for her service and dedication during her time working for The Government of St. Maarten. Albertina was also remembered for her work she did at the Cole Bay Methodist Church, where she worshipped. On Sunday February 22nd. 2010 she was honored on her 78th. Birthday. Some of the Members sang songs that she taught them while they were in the Young Adventures and at Sunday School. Sister Linda Piper, one of her musical students, accompanied them on the organ. Sister Irma James Richardson now deceased made a speech regarding her memories of Albertina, then sang the song that she taught her during her Sunday School days. She said "Quote on quote:" Teacher was the one who found out that I had a beautiful voice and made me practice this song for during a Sunday Morning Worship." Irma had been blessing people with singing for The Lord Jesus Christ ever since then, and Albertina always looked forward in hearing her sing that particular song for her on her birthday. Sister Vernice David also made a speech about her memories of Teacher when she was growing up. Albertina was moved and was very happy, especially when she was told that her former music class student Linda Piper, accompanied the group of singers by playing the piano. She was presented with gifts and a lovely bouquet of flowers from all of them. Teacher thanked them wholeheartedly. The Youth Choir lead by Sis. Berthille Chittick, aka "Teacher Betty," also sang for Albertina and presented her with a lovely gift.

The Church School and members of the Church continued to visit Sister Albertina Joe at her home after she was unable to attend Church.

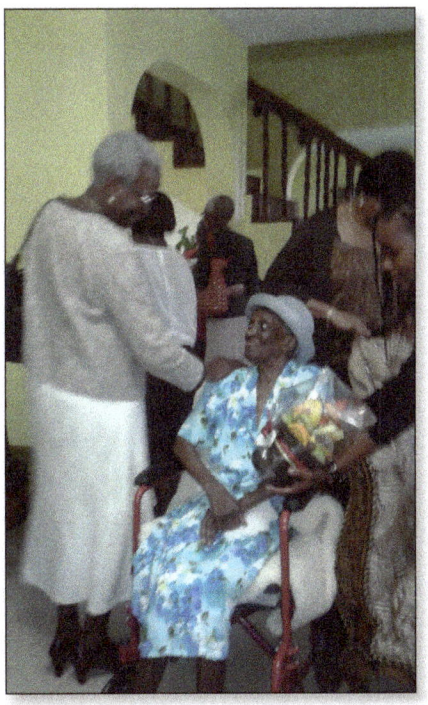

Photos of teacher's birthday celebration

Albertina Joe's Family Tree:

Names:	Relations:
Ernest Joe	Father
Joseph Joe	Grandfather
Caroline Peters	Grandmother
Leonora Joe a.k.a. Miss Lilly	Mother
Williams Laveist	Grandfather
Mary Anne Laveist	Grandmother
James Laveist	Uncle
Eulalie Joe	Sister
Mona Joe	Niece

The Family Joe, Mr. Ernest and Mrs. Leonora Joe with their daughters: Eulalie and Albertina Joe.

CHAPTER 2

Some names of Ministers, Local Preachers, church school Teachers, and students during Albertina's tenure

Ministers

Name of Methodist Ministers	Years Served:	Place of Birth:
Rev. C. Leonard Carty	1951–1955	Anguilla
Rev. Perkins	1951–1955	England
Rev. Franklin Roberts	1955–1958	Anguilla
Rev. Trevor Bates	1955–1958	England
Rev. George Ambler	1957–1958	
Rev. Frank Wilby a.k.a Willerby	1958–1962	England
Rev. Kenrick M. Khan	1960–1964	Guyana
Rev. Albert Moffett	1964–1969	Ireland
Rev. Reginald Willingham	1969–1971	
Rev. John A. Gumbs	1971–1977	Anguilla
Rev. Lloyd Brissett	1969–1972 1988–1994	Jamaica
Rev. Melboune Bailey	1972–1974	Jamaica

Rev. Halley Marville	1974–1976	Barbados
Rev. Peterson Joseph	1976–1977	Antigua
Rev. Dr. Birchfield Aymer	1977–1979	Antigua
Rev. G. Nichols	1977–1978	Antigua
Rev. Raymond Nielly	1978–1979	Turks and Caicos Isl.
Rev. Moise Isidore	1979–1982	Haiti
Rev. Dr. Wilfred Hodge	1979–1983	Anguilla
Rev. Roger Decker	1982–1984	
Rev. Neil Drayton	1990–1992	

Sis. Albertina continued to correspond with some of the ministers after they left the shores of St. Maarten.

Below is a photo of Rev. Franklin Roberts and his family

Local preachers
- Sis. Eulalie Meyers
- Bro. Nathaniel Richardson
- Sis. Glorine Richardson
- Mr. Samuel James
- Bro. Teclo Bell
- Bro. Osborne James
- Bro. Francisco Sherwood
- Bro. Richard Hazel
- Sis. Mildred James
- Bro. Vincent James
- Sis. Browlia Millard
- Bro. Ernest Gibbs
- Sis. Catherine de Weever
- Sis. Rose Miller

Church School Teachers
- Sis. Christine Rombley
- Sis. Adina Bell
- Sis. Mildred Rochester
- Bro. Tony Jacobs
- Bro. Sylvio Lammar a.k.a Phelps and Linda Piper,

Church School Students

Linda Piper, Ruth Nisbeth, Cynthia Nisbeth, Doris Payne, Muriel Reed, Angelica Reed, Ingrid Reed, Elcita Reed, Emma Bell Winter, Dianne Bell (deceased), Russell

Bell, Van Dijk Bell, Allen Reed, George Reed(Deceased), Louis Laveist, Carl Aventurin (deceased), Agnes Aventurin, Mary Aventurin, Mona Richardson, Iona Richardson and Gloria Richardson-Bryson, Germaine Richardson, Elton Richardson, James Richardson a.k.a. "Jamesy" (deceased). Louis Maccow, Leroy Maccow, Monica Richardson, Irma Richardson-James, Victor Richardson, Vernice David, Mona Maccow-Joe, Beverly Rochester, and many more.

CHAPTER 3

Some History of Methodism in Sint Maarten

In 1817, the seed of Methodism was sown. John Hodge and his friends from Anguilla introduced Methodism to French Saint Martin. He was driven by the Holy Spirit to spread the Gospels and the good news about the power of Jesus Christ throughout the island. He frequently crossed the waters between Anguilla and Saint Martin. The missionaries conducted crowded and successful evangelistic meetings in Marigot, the capital of the French territory. They preached mainly to the slaves but were unfortunately expelled by French authorities. Only French-speaking missionaries were allowed to preach there. The missionaries had to flee to Cole Bay, the Dutch territory of the Twin-island.

Cole Bay Methodist Church. (The Bedrock)

John Hodge started preaching the Gospel under a tamarind tree on the property near the current Cole Bay Methodist Chapel. His message gained popularity among those who embraced the teachings of Christ. However, Hodge and his followers faced resistance from people who disagreed with their "fire-and-brimstone preaching. Undeterred by the opposition, they continued to hold worship services, even though they were sometimes disrupted. Their opponents used horsewhips to disband the group of believers. But regardless of this, the number of converts continued to increase. Seeing the need for a permanent place to worship, the first Methodist Chapel was built in **1829** at the present location in Cole Bay. It was a wooden two-story structure. Today, Cole Bay Methodist Church is known for the bedrock of Sint Maarten.

The first 2 story Cole Bay Methodist Church building, taken from the Philipsburg Church office gallery

As the Gospel of Salvation spread from the Cole Bay area, more and more persons from Philipsburg (the Dutch capital) and other communities attended the missionary services. Freedom of religious worship was not allowed at that time, so persons disguised themselves when attending the services.

Louisiana Illidge, "Mother of Methodism," and 11 churches

Sister Louisiana Agusta Illidge strengthened Methodism in Philipsburg. Her genuine and unwavering commitment to spreading the Gospel earned her the respected title "Mother of Methodism". She was devoted and committed to her faith, and her efforts were so instrumental in promoting it that the brick building was named after her at the Philipsburg Methodist Church Ground. This building still stands in its original form as a testament to her contribution. Since then many Methodist churches have been built on both the French and Dutch sides of the island. The French Sint Martin Circuit used to have five Methodist churches, but unfortunately, one was completely destroyed by a hurricane, leaving them with only four. Similarly, the Dutch side has seven Methodist churches that continue to progress well. Most of Cole Bay inhabitants were Methodists; however, many other denominations have been established in the village since then.

Cited from the 197th Conference of the Leeward islands District St. Maarten/St. Martin Circuit dated January 20th to 31st 2003 booklet page 19

Highlights of Methodism in Cole Bay

Ministers came from as far as England and Ireland with their families to pastor the Methodist churches in these islands. The chapel was always filled during Sunday morning worship. People loved to worship on Sundays; the children loved to attend Sunday school and take part in different activities in the church. Seeing there weren't much distractions away from church, children faithfully attended young people meeting on Friday nights. Young people meetings were the place where every young person was happy to be at. In the past, when the Methodist Church School ended, some students attended church schools belonging to other denominations. Others would visit their loved ones and friends or stroll in the village. However, they were required to return home before sunset.

In the Methodist Churches, several groups existed, including the Women's League, Men's Fellowship, Young Adventures, Classes, Boys and Girls Brigade, Church School, and Church Choirs, each with its leader. The leaders of the classes were responsible for leading around twelve individuals per class and held weekly meetings to discuss challenges, read scriptures, pray, sing, and support one another. If a problem exceeded the leader's knowledge, they consulted the Pastor. If a church member fell ill or passed away, the leader or their family notified the Pastor. The Pastor took the initiative to make home visits to ensure the welfare of the congregation. In Cole Bay, there are still existing class systems, except for the Boys and Girls Brigade. However, new organizations have emerged and are now active. The Cole Bay Methodist Church has organized several entertaining events, including concerts, bazaars, pageants, and competitions, which were all well-received by the participants.

Written by: Agnes Aventurin

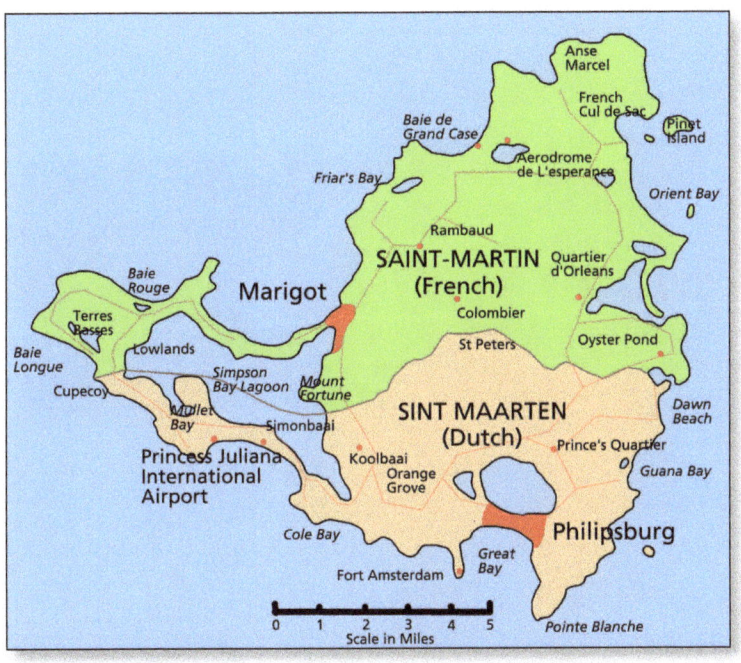

Map of Sint Maarten/Saint-Martin

Coat of Arms/Flag of Sint Maarten

CHAPTER 4

SOME HISTORICAL INFORMATION ABOUT ST. MAARTEN

Sint Maarten is a little island in the Caribbean, measures 37 square miles and is divided into two parts: the Dutch side (South) and the French side (North). Although so small, it is governed by two entities. The Dutch side of the island is a constituent country in the Kingdom of the Netherlands in the Caribbean and measures 16 square miles. The French side became an overseas collectivity of France in 2007 rather than a colony. It covers an area of 21 square miles. It is known as "The Friendly island". There were long stretches of beautiful Stone Walls alongside the streets of both French and Dutch side of the island. which were erected by slaves. Sint Maarten/Saint Martin houses a variety of ethnic groups with different backgrounds. People from all around the world, including various islands and countries, come to live here. There is a Monument at the Frontiers revealing both sides of the island, the Flamboyant is our National Tree. The Brown Pelican is our National bird, the national flower is the Yellow Sage. The St. Maarten

Flag is Red, White and blue. Our island has two airports: "Princess Juliana International Airport" on the Dutch side, and "L'Espérance Airport" bka Grand Case Airport on the French side. The Princess Juliana International Airport is a hub for different destinations. Previously, we had four official holidays in addition to the religious ones. These four were Queen Juliana's Birthday, celebrated on April 30th, Labour Day on May 1st, Sint Maarten's Day on November 11th, and Kingdom Day on December 15th.

Queen's Birthday is now replaced by Kings Day and is celebrated on April 30th. Additionally, Emancipation Day has taken the place of Kingdom Day. Two additional holidays have been added to the Calendar: Emancipation Day on July 1st and Constitution Day on October 10th. It's worth noting that Constitution Day is observed every second Monday in October.

The name of our Sint Maarten song, is "O sweet Saint Maarten Land", is sung on both sides of our island for special occasions; the original song was written by Father Gerard Kemps. Pristine clear blue waters encompass the shores of Sint Maarten and are surrounded with picturesque white glistening sandy beaches.

There are several routes one can take to get to their destination on the island. However, the streets in the village of Cole Bay are mainly used to travel back and forth to the French and Dutch parts of the island.

The Dawn of Electricity in Sint Maarten

When I was a little girl, the island's electricity was stored manually, but we must acknowledge the tremendous effort it took to provide this essential service. I vividly remember watching the dedicated employees of GEBE who worked tirelessly to bring electricity to Cole Bay. They used various tools, such as picks, hoes, crowbars, and shovels, to dig holes for the poles that would line the streets. Installing these tall poles was no easy feat, as the workers had to climb them to install the upper wiring for the street lights. Safety was paramount, and so the workers wore wide belts around their waist and the poles, attaching hooks to their safety shoes while climbing. Their hard work was necessary to bring electricity to our island.

After the Princess Juliana Airport opened, airplanes only flew into Sint Maarten during the daytime. The workers faced even more significant challenges when planting poles in the hills to provide lights at the top for nighttime landings. They manually cleared tracks from the streets to the top of the hills by chopping down trees, cacti, and brushes. Climbing the poles to hook the overhead cables on each pole until they reached the top was no easy feat. Only then could they install the red lights at the top of the hills. Without their hard work, airplanes may not have been able to land on the island at night until an alternative solution was found.

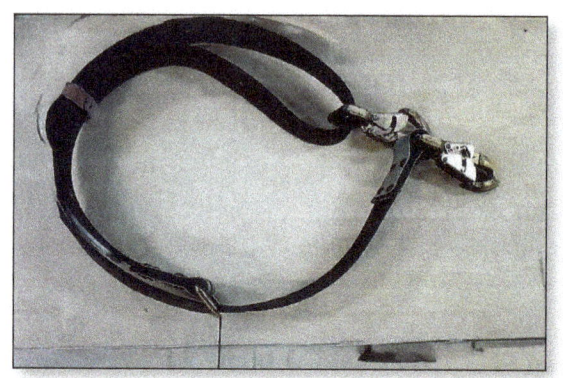

Safety Belt Extension

Safety Belt

Chapter 5

Cole Bay, a Close-Knit Population

Cole Bay is a little village where up until the 1970s everyone knew each other, looked out for one another and helped each other in whatever way they could. It was a handful of loving and caring people. Everyone shared what he or she reaped from their gardens with each other. If a person ran out of sugar or any item while cooking food, they ran to the next-door neighbor to ask for some of theirs if they had the extra. Their behavior showcased the strong bond they shared. During Christmas, people prepared homemade pastries, tarts, cakes, puddings, and drinks and shared them.

Parents left their children at home with the assurance that the neighbor would look out for their children while they were out working, or the eldest child of the siblings would look out for the younger ones. The children could not pass anyone by without giving the greetings of the day. If they did, you can bet your last dollar that your parent knew it before he/she got home, and you would be spanked or disciplined for not having any manners. If a child did anything wrong and a grownup witnessed it, they were permitted to correct the child or even spank them once they did not take advantage of them.

People did over-the-counter shopping, or through the windows of the shopkeepers' homes. They purchased items by the pound, kilo, ounce, gallon, or liter. Butter, Cheese or Lard was weighed in Brown paper bags on the measuring scale and sold for a price.

Up to in the early 50's the streets of Cole Bay were unpaved; there were few vehicles and no streetlights. People used lamps or lanterns to see at night. One or two families had kerosine refrigerators and stoves in their homes. Those that did not have any would get or purchase a mug of ice from someone who owned a fridge in the community. It was normal for people to include an extra plate of food while they were cooking just in case someone passed by for a visit, they could offer them a meal. Some Families always provided an extra plate of food for a less fortunate child. That child benefitted considerably because sometimes a plate of food is saved by more than one home for him/her.

People who didn't own a cistern received a bucket or two of drinking water from a neighbor who owned one especially during drought. Some women took drinking water to their homes by carrying a bucket of water on their heads while carrying one in each of their hands. The water caught in drums around the house was for domestic use and baths. Sundays were and still are special days; the majority of families on

St. Maarten prepared their elaborate tasty meals for breakfast, lunch, and dinner, relaxed in the afternoon, or went for long Sunday afternoon strolls and visited neighbours, family and friends.

Bathrooms were built at the back of most homes. A clean oil drum was placed on the top of the roof: Pipe fittings were attached from the cistern to the tank and a shower faucet was attached to it from the inside of the bathroom. The water was pumped manually up to the tank that was on the roof. Families who could not afford that type of indoor luxury, build a little galvanize room at the back of their homes and had their baths by using plastic pails of water. Persons used yellow or blue soap to bathe with, while others knew of certain bushes that would lather and used that to bathe with instead.

Outhouses were built a distant away from the homes. They were not designed for flushing waste. It stored litter and was kept covered when not in use.

Before there were wash machines, persons soaked their clothes with soap water in a big bath-pan over night and washed the following morning with their hands or scrubbed their laundry on scrubbing boards.

Scrub board

Soaking clothes overnight, enabled the people to wash easier. The washboard was considered a luxury in the earlier days before 1960's, as not everyone could afford washboards. Some were made with fluted tin, sheet iron, copper or zinc, framed within a board. Later on, washboards were made of glass. Washing by hand was a long process. White clothes were put in the sun on the line to bleach, and then rinsed in a tub with blue water. Cotton or linen shirts, skirts, dresses and pants were soaked in starch water. This starched water caused the clothes to become very stiff when they were dry. (This starch was cooked before it was used in the clothes).

Back in the day, clothes were washed with blue soap. When the starched clothes were ready to iron, each garment would be sprinkled with water, rolled up individually for a while and then ironed. White Cotton Clothes were also boiled in Copper pots or big pans.

As was mentioned earlier, there was no electricity before the early 1960s in Cole Bay. People did not have much choice and raised pigs, cows, sheep, goats, and chickens in their backyards. Some of the eggs from the chickens were left to hatch, and some were used to eat or sell. Likewise, the goats, cows and sheep. They were handled the same manner as the fowls. Persons who owned their own animals, milked their goats but mostly the cows, and sold it by the bottles and made their own cheese and butter from the cream of the milk. They scalded the milk before drinking it. Animals were butchered, so their families would have meat to eat. Fishermen came from the village of Simpson Bay throughout the village of Cole Bay and sold their fish by the strap. The fishermen used a conch shell to alert people in the villages that they were in the area. Lobsters were often used as bait to catch fish or given away to customers. Today, Lobster is one of the most expensive meal on menus, one can hardly afford it. In the past, families without kerosene refrigerators would fry and eat their fish immediately or save them for the next day. To preserve other meats like pork and beef, they would use sea salt to cure them and hang them outside to dry until they were ready to be cooked. This was how they kept their food from spoiling. The corned meat, or fish, were soaked overnight and sometime boiled, to ensure the excess salt was extracted from it. This is the same procedure used at present with Saltfish and or corned Pork. Most of the people owned their own vegetable gardens, season gardens and lots of local fruit trees in their backyards or in the hills.

Before everyone owned a stove, they used stone ovens to bake their breads, cooked outside on three stones, or used cold pots.

Ancient Baking Oven

Persons who knew how to bake on three stones also baked Johnny cakes or cake that way. They positioned the lighted wood between the opening of three stones, then placed the big iron pot on top of it when the wood burned sufficiently. It was customary for persons to put a galvanize over the Iron pot and place some of the burned wood on the top of it. When the pot heated to a certain temperature, the person would put the cake batter in a baking pan and place it in an iron pot to bake their cakes or Johnnycakes.

CHAPTER 6

MY STORY ABOUT SIS. ALBERTINA JOE A.K.A. "TEACHER"

I grew up in the village of Cole Bay, not far away from the Cole Bay Methodist Church, and I can clearly remember Teacher: full of life and peppy, traversing back and forth to the Cole Bay Methodist Church, doing God's business with pleasure. I must have taken her for granted, because I did not understand the sacrifices, she made to do the work she did in the church, besides her everyday chores. However, from all the other Sunday School teachers, she was the one that stood out most for me.

When some of the other teachers did not show up for Sunday School, teacher was always there. I can barely remember the other teachers in my time, but if there were any, there were none like Teacher. Besides my mother, teacher was the one who taught me the Word of God, Sunday School songs, and read us Bible stories. When my siblings and I got home from Sunday School, we were expected to recite the memory verse to my mother and tell her what we learned. After certain lessons, Teacher would tell us we had to get ourselves ready, for God was coming soon for His world; and she would advise us if we were not ready, to start doing so. She would ask us which way we wanted to go, to heaven or hell. I was just a little girl and my mind began racing; This, I could hardly comprehend. I talked to myself; if Jesus comes, my dreams would be shattered. I will never get a chance to marry, have children or build my dream home: there goes my blueprint for my future.

This information from her was quickly dismissed from my mind as I left Sunday School. I did not understand how we were to prepare ourselves for the coming of the Lord. Now I understand it is building a personal relationship with God: obeying Him, talking with Him regularly, focusing on His Word and emulating Jesus by reaching out to others. Especially those who are in need. It's about being a living example to others by doing what is right in the sight of God and sharing his Holy Word. After all, this is what Teacher did; she remained focus. Maybe if Teacher did get married, she would not have been able to do all she did in her time. She would be distracted from leading us to Christ. The Apostle Paul says in 1 Timothy 4:16 (GWT), *"Focus on your lives and your teachings, continue to do what I have told you. If you do this, you will save yourself and those who hear you."*

Maybe Teacher explained what she meant when she said God is coming soon, but my mind was racing during her explanation; so I must have been in my own little world, trying to figure out why God is going to end the world without my dreams being fulfilled. I remember also thinking that Jerusalem and Egypt were in heaven when she told us the stories about Jesus. All those places mentioned in the Bible were in heaven, according to me, not here on earth.

Church school commenced at 3 pm on Sundays and ended at 5 pm. Teacher was also doing so many other things in the church and did not receive a penny for her services, but God will reward her one day. I believe there is a special place for her up in heaven. Teacher had plenty of tolerance; I can't tell you that she ever had an attitude toward us, although we were very disgusting as children. I can remember when we were disobedient, she would keep scolding us and one of her favourite words, when we didn't listen to her, was **"Confound you, Child"**. During our present Sunday Morning Worship, Teacher still unconsciously used her fingers on the pew in front of her as if she was playing the organ while the congregation was singing. I never knew how much I admired this lady until now that I am grown and is also a Sunday School teacher and leading other organisations in the church.

It takes a lot of time and endurance to keep on going, day after day. Teacher is no longer with us, but I can imagine hearing her saying to me, "I am still around with a big smile on her face. Besides my few mentors who impacted my life from my early childhood, teacher Albertina was one I looked up to, and I will always lovingly remember her throughout my life. It took a humble woman of tiny stature with a great character to make a difference in the lives of many. It is really said that a good leader should be a good example; she displayed whatever she taught. 1st. Timothy 4:12 (NIV) says, *"Don't let anyone look down on you because you are young, but set an example for the believers in speech, in conduct, in love, in faith and in purity.* Teacher never mislead anyone and if she did, I wasn't aware of it. She has been a good example to all of us in the church as well as on the streets. (Matthew 18:6, NRSV: *"If any of you put a stumbling block before one of these little ones who believe in me, it would be better for you if a great millstone were fastened around your neck and you were drowned in the depth of the sea."*)

There are many ways members and leaders can expose others to temptations and enticements, which could cause them to sin. As Christians, we must be careful what we say or do. At times, people quit the church because of how we treat them. They don't feel welcomed, or they hear someone whispering something about him/her. Many times, we preach one thing and do the opposite, or hinder the young Christian from growing in the Word. Teacher, in my sight, is a living example of a child of God who did not mislead anyone. She walked with her head high and brought others to Christ.

Teacher followed the desires of our Heavenly Father and worked all for the glory of Him. She did as the Bible says, *"Let your light shine before others, so that they may see your good works and give glory to your Father in heaven"* (Matt. 5:16, NRSV).

She had no time for things of the world but has prepared her life and soul for God. Teacher knew that all that she owned here on earth was just temporary, but to be with Christ is for eternity.

I trust that as I continue my journey with Christ, and continue serving Him, that I too, will make a difference in people's lives by being a good example and bringing them closer to Christ as Teacher did.

Agnes Aventurin

Blurps

Sister Agnes, as she is called by her fellow congregants, is a devoted believer of Jesus Christ who has passionately debated her convictions of her faith and belief in God. She loves the youth and is committed to their personal and spiritual development. As a Christian educator, she ensures that the little ones of the faith are spiritually nurtured as they encounter God as He is revealed in worship at the Cole Bay Methodist Church. Her passion for biblical knowledge and how the Caribbean Methodist church traditions have evolved led her to document the faith responses and experiences of St. Maarten Methodist stalwarts. It is my pleasure to commend this book to you trusting that it offers insights towards strengthening your commitment and relationship with God.

Patmore C. Henry Pastor

My close interaction with Sis. Agnes R. Aventurin has been for about two and a half years now and within that short period of time I can say the following about her character.

- Meticulous in everything she does.

- Very inspiring in giving her life stories.
- Great conversationalist.
- Straightforward.
- She may not be well understood if you don't have the same compassion as her for everyday things in life.

It was no surprise to me when I learned that she was busy writing a book. Such talent should never be kept in the dark.

Renny E. Duzon

Agnes is a determined and dedicated individual, who passionately fulfills her divine purpose. She is loving, compassionate and doesn't think twice to give of herself unselfishly when there is a need. She believes in and encourages children and young people alike to be all that they are created and destined to be.

Ruth P. Pratt Pastor

Interviewees

Miss Albertina Joe aka Teacher (February 22, 1932 to October 06, 2017)
Mr. Carlos Patrick (head of the Land Registry on St. Maarten)
Mr. Neville Lake, a.k.a. Doc
Mr. Godwin James (deceased)
Ms. Felicia James (deceased)
Mrs. Elcita Atkins
Ms. Mona Maccow-Joe
Ms. Louisa Halley
Mr. Gaston Bell

Citations

Book entitled: ***Disciple.*** *Becoming Disciples through Bible Study* by Richard Byrd Wilke and Julia Kitchens Wilke, **"God uses the simple to show faith and love".** (**ISBN 13: 978-0-687-78349-6 Study Manual, copyright 1993 by Abingdon Press**)

History -Windward island Bank St. Maarten https://www.wib-bank.net Info:

Philipsburg Methodist Chapel 160ᵗʰ years booklet 1851 to 2011: Names of Ministers who served both Dutch and French congregations.

Information Cited on results of "Hurricane Frederic" (from Hurricanecentral.freeservers.com/subtitle Casualty and damage Statistics. "7 deaths were reported in Sint Maarten".)

A Short History of St. Maarten booklet by the St. Maarten Heritage Foundation:

- The first Airport on Sint Maarten opened in 1943

Methodism in the earlies: History of the beginning of the Cole Bay Methodist Church and List of past MCCA Ministers. **Information cited from the 197th Conference of the Leeward Islands Districts St. Maarten/St. Martin Circuit dated January 20th to January 31st, 2003, magazine page 19.:**

Philipsburg Methodist Chapel 160th years booklet 1851 to 2011 Page 30. Published by: The Philipsburg Methodist Church St. Maarten- Dutch Caribbean.

- Ministers who served in the St. Maarten/St. Martin Circuit 1819 – 2011) printed 2011

Methodist Hymn Book with Offices: Copyright, December 1933. (The text and Biographical details have been revised to April 1954.

Enquiries regarding this book should be sent to Methodist Publishing House 20 Ivatt Way, Peterborough PE3 7PG England. Printed and bounded in England by MPG BOOKS LTD, BODMIN CORNWALL

- Hymn nr. 538: *"What a friend we have in Jesus."* Page # 206. (Author: Joseph Medlicott Scriven, 1820-86.)

- Hymn nr. 390: "Give me the Faith which can remove." Page nr. #150 (Author: Charles Wesley. 1707-88,)

Bible Readings

Psalm 121: I will lift up mine eyes unto the hills, from whence cometh my help (king James Version)

Ruth 1: 16,17: Entreat me not to leave thee, or to return from following after thee for wither thou goest I will go (King James Version)

1st Timothy 4:16 Focus in your lives and your teaching. Continue to do what I have told you. If you do this, you will save yourself and those who hear you. (GWT)

1st Timothy 4:12 Don't let anyone look down on you, because you are young, but set an example for the believers… (NIV)

Mathew 18:6 If anyone of you put a stumbling block before these children who believe in me… (NRSV)

Mathew 5:16 Let your light so shine before men, that they may see your good works and glorify your father which is in heaven. (NRSV)

Pictures

Picture of the 1st Airport building on St. Maarten: **The brief history compiled by the St. Maarten National Heritage Foundation and the St. Maarten Museum**

Pictures of the 1st Cole Bay Methodist Church 2 story building: **from the Philipsburg Methodist Church offices gallery.**

Picture from: **Protected Historical sites and buildings on St. Maarten produced by Vromi**

- Picture of the Cole Bay old public School, "Leonard Connor school"

Picture from Brochure on the St. Maarten Government Monument first group,

- Photo of the signal Master houses on Fort Amsterdam

Pictures Received from Sis. Albertine Joe; Rev. Franklin Roberts & Fam., Rev. Willerby & fam., Herself and her family.

Pictures from Felicia James: Mrs. Lucille Hazel and information concerning Women's League in Cole Bay.

Pictures taken by Mrs. Elcita Atkins:

- The Leopold Bell School, formerly known as the Leonard Conner School in its present state.
- The old stone oven from the back yard of the Maccow's property, next to the Leonard Conner School

Mr. Franklin Peters:

- Picture taken of the remains of the Well in Well Road, Cole Bay.

Zénia Cannegieter: Pictures of the present Cole Bay Methodist Church. The original church Bell, The Coal Pot, The Irons or goose, Wash board.

Mr. Lancelot Kennedy Thompson: The Scale and weights:

Ms. Masie Richardson & Kaye Henderson: Foto of Kerosine Lamps

Mr. Hubert Pantophlet: the goose.

Online image: Map of Sint Maarten/St. Martin

Pictures of old slave walls in Colombier, French St. Maarten on Front and back cover of this Book, by **Lancelot Kennedy Thompson of "Kennedy's photo studio" in Philipsburg St. Maarten.**

Pictures taken by Eugene Abram of the Belts and its extension.

Author's Biography

Agnes Aventurin was born in French Saint Martin and raised in the village of Cole Bay, along with her six siblings. She is the daughter of the late Clementina Aventurin and Arthur Aventurin. She received her education on the island of Sint Maarten and is a firm believer in Christ. Agnes has been a Church School teacher for over 27 years, including ten years as a Superintendent, and was also a Class leader in the Cole Bay Methodist Church. She produces a daily Bible reading program under the umbrella of the Sint Maarten Methodist Circuit Facebook page and UTUBE.

Agnes has always been passionate about writing and reading; this is her first book. She strongly believes in "rising above life struggles and becoming an overcomer." After working with the Electric Company NV GEBE for over 40 years, she is now retired and enjoys spending quality time with her family and friends. She amuses herself with gardening, home improvements, listening to music, storytelling, and writing.

Agnes is the parent of two grown children and a grandmother of four. She has made her home in South Reward.

Printed in the USA
CPSIA information can be obtained
at www.ICGtesting.com
LVHW060028050324
773527LV00010B/64